GIVING BIRTH TO PURPOSE IN AN UNCOMFORTABLE PLACE

Salome Williams

Book completion services provided by
TRU Statement Publications
www.trustatementpublications.com

First Printing: 2019
ISBN: 13: 978-1-948085-27-4

Luke 2 vs 7

And she brought forth her firstborn son, and wrapped him in swaddling clothes, and laid him in a manger; because there was no room for them in the inn.

Salome Williams

DEDICATION

This book is dedicated to the underserved, underappreciated, unwanted, ridiculed, unthanked, unloved, unvalued, uncherished, underprivileged, penurious, the abused, rejected, forsaken, disliked, despised, detested, undesired, forsaken, neglected, ignored, outcast, unwelcomed, shunned, abhorred, isolated, homeless, unattached, deserted, lonely, down-hearted, despaired, scorned, outcast, depressed, oppressed...

I Corinthians 1 vs 28-31 (NIV)
God chose the lowly things-and the despised things-and the thigs that are not- to nullify the things that are, so that no man may boast before him. It is because of him that you are in Christ Jesus, who became for us the wisdom from God-that is, our righteousness, holiness and redemption. Therefore, as it is written: Let the one who boasts, boast in the Lord."

You are known, you are loved, and you have a purpose.

Salome Williams

ACKNOWLEDGEMENTS

Thanking my heavenly Father, our Lord and Savior Jesus Christ, who has given, reminded, ignited, highlighted, and lifted inside of me the purpose He has ordained for me, from my mother's womb.

Thank you to my amazing husband, Alrick Williams, who sacrificed precious time and resources to help me in writing this book. I learnt so much about the process of marriage, just by our union. Marriage can be rough at times, but I thank God for you. There were nights when you were left sleeping alone for a few hours while I stayed up writing in the living room, but you understood the importance of the quiet time I needed in the late midnight hours, in order to have a clear mind and understanding of what God wanted me to share in this book. Thank you also for allowing me to share some intimate portions of our marriage with the purpose of helping someone else along their process.

My son, Ajani Williams, who was ignored many times just so I could focus on writing, thank you for tolerating all my frustrations during this process.

I want to specially thank my mother, Stephany Nelson, for being the initial example in my earlier life as a child. Thank you for reminding me of who I am and who God has created me to be.

Thank you to my father, Delroy Nelson, who pushed me to think big, want big, but also not to forget those who are often times forgotten. One of your favorite sayings was,

"Don't forget the principal thing."

I interpreted this saying as,

"Don't forget the small things, not the least of the ones who helped me to where I am and where I want to go."

Don't forget the unforgotten.

How can I forget my late grandfather, who was my old friend and farming partner when I was little? I didn't have many friends, and you would take the time to talk with me and make me smile, even though I was normally quiet. You saw everything good in me, even though I was flawed. Thank you for encouraging me. R.I.P grandpa. I love you and miss you.

Many thanks to all of my family, friends, and acquaintances who have ever imparted something into me. Many of whom I have just looked at how they lived their lives and it made a great impact on my life.

Thank you to those of you who treated me unkind. You unknowingly helped me, and now I am helping others.

Thank you to my previous and current church family, who has shown me love and support in countless ways.

Thank you all.

TABLE OF CONTENTS

INTRODUCTION

Giving Birth to Purpose in an Uncomfortable Place, was written to remind, inspire, motivate, and encourage all my readers in the understanding, *God has given each and every one of you a purpose before you were born.*

This book was written from an uncomfortable place. I realized, even today, that many times I feel like I'm not what I should be, and I am less than what I truly am. To be totally honest, I found it difficult to write about a lot of things in my life, because of the fear of reexperiencing the emotions of how I felt when I was younger. Many times, you will feel inhibited in expressing yourself, even with the folks that are closest to you.

According to many national polls and statistics, our schools and churches are named among the highest to place judgement on particular groups of people. Even without words, this can be palpable.

The school system is designed so that we are to apply to schools, and even if you have good grades and no criminal record, they still complete additional searches on where you lived and perhaps your family history. As to say, that your place of upbringing and family history has anything to do with you moving forward in bettering yourself.

In some churches, most of the condemnation begins upon the entrance into the sanctuary. There is a silent judgement of what you look like, how you dress, the color of your skin, and your level of education. As if, God's prevenient grace is all about the outward appearance of an individual.

People are often left behind in our society if their status is not up to par with their status of hierarchy. The individuals who are most often looked down on and are made to feel they have no sense of purpose, are usually the few who have something of value to offer when given the chance. The purpose and the anointing on their lives is truly what will make a difference in their own lives and even the lives of the one who condemns them. Unfortunately, in most, the intellectual has taken over and the lack of Wisdom has been pushed to the side.

The purpose of this book is that it will assist in taking you through the *process to purpose*, and teach you how to overcome the obstacles that prevent you from rising into what God has truly placed in you before you were born, with the determination of bringing purpose out of you.

Perhaps the place where you were born, or where you are currently placed, whether physically and mentally, may not have been conducive to giving birth to what God has truly placed on the inside of you. Perhaps what others have said about you has made you feel like you have no purpose, or they have said many things to hurt you, to stunt your growth and development into your true potential.

Regardless of which statement is true for you, please be reminded that Jesus, The Christ, who was born in a manger because there was no room for Him in the inn, became the savior of the whole world. He too was rejected by men, talked about, made to feel less than, because of where he was born, how he grew up, what he ate, and so on.

Perhaps the difficulties you have gone through, the circumstances surrounding your earlier life, or where you grew up, was not all you wanted or hoped for; nevertheless, you can make today the day when you shake off all the negative thoughts, hold your head high, be brave, and stand up for yourself and what is right. You also have an opportunity to use what you stand for to give others a voice until they are able to speak for themselves. No longer will you stand around and allow people to make others feel like they are not important, as if they don't have a purpose and serve as one. It's time to be a voice and change generations.

Be an advocate. What's in you will have a generational effect and move others to a place of purpose. Most importantly remember, you can *give birth to purpose in an uncomfortable place.*

Don't just exist, LIVE!!!

Salome Williams

CHAPTER 1
PURSUING PURPOSE

1Kings 19 vs 19-21 (KJV)

"So he departed thence, and found Elisha the son of Shaphat, who was plowing with twelve yoke of oxen before him, and he with the twelfth: and Elijah passed by him, and cast his mantle upon him. And he left the oxen, and ran after Elijah, and said, let me, I pray thee, kiss my father and my mother, and then I will follow thee.

And he said unto him, Go back again: for what have I done to thee? And he returned back from him, and took a yoke of oxen, and slew them, and boiled their flesh with the instruments of the oxen, and gave unto the people, and they did eat. Then he arose, and went after Elijah, and ministered unto him."

According to the American journalist and bestselling author Rich Kalgaard, *a purpose is a soft virtue, but it's what gives you steel in your spine.*

It is hard to really see what your purpose is in this 21st century, when most of us, perhaps all of us, are so distracted by the many things that are happening in our lives and around us.

Often times, even though we are pressed, encouraged, and called to something that is greater than us, we fail to realize what is truly within us, because we are preoccupied with everything else around us.

There is something within you that you do well, and with the least effort. Having the zeal to know it, and understand it, will push you towards expanding that *something* on a larger spectrum.

Getting out from behind the veils of your past and present environment, whether it is physical and/or mental, will allow yourself to see your true potential. You will be surprised of the great gift and purpose God has truly placed inside of you, to manifest outside of you, and for His glory.

Elijah left what was comfortable and went after something, that even though it wasn't comfortable, compared to what he was used to, he knew that in the end, it would be so much more than what he had.

> ### When comfortable, becomes uncomfortable.

MY PRAYER FOR YOU

Father God, I honor you and am grateful for a time such as this. You have given us great things to be in expectation of. I thank you that this reader has followed you in a path of purpose. You have called them into great purpose for your will and glorification. I pray the purpose of promises of the mantel you have placed your son and daughter is felt, and they start on their journey toward Promise. Father I pray, that your Spirit will dwell in them, and they rely on your leading as they take each step of faith. I pray a covering over your children in Jesus name. I pray a new awareness in their senses. I pray their eyes are fixed on you, and as they grow in the course, they are aware of what is healthy and unhealthy for their process. I pray a hedge of protection around them in Jesus name. I pray against all distractions in their lives, and I pray for a daily renewing of the mind of Christ, that they be not moved from the place of process, but stay steadfast in the way you lead them. In Jesus name I/we pray and are grateful that you have chosen them to do something great things for you. Amen.

PURSUING PURPOSE

Below are questions to answer regarding Pursuing Purpose. Use the pages at the end of this chapter or a separate journal to record and reflect on your answers, as you journey through your process.

1. Do you understand what purpose you are in pursuit of?
2. Have you embraced or denied your purpose? Explain your embrace or denial.
3. Has God sent someone to you to help you in your journey?
4. Have you given up things or people in order to start your process to purpose? If so, list the things you have released, and if not, list the people or things you are afraid to let go.
5. Is this your first attempt in pursuing purpose? If not explain what happened.

YOUR PRAYER FOR PURPOSE

Father God, I give you the glory, the honor, and the praise. I am grateful that you have chosen me. You have planted a seed of purpose in my heart, and I pray your nurturing hand over it. I am thankful for the purpose you have placed in me, whether I am fully aware of it or not, I am assured you have called me to serve you. I pray you reveal the depths of my purpose as I faithful walk in my process. I ask your forgiveness for denying any part of what you have called me to be. If I have rejected the mantel placed on my life, I know I have rejected you. I pray for your divine connection for those who you have had chosen to walk alongside me in my process. I am grateful that there are people who will encourage me. They will see and hear You, in all that I do, and I will not harden my heart to any correction or adjustments they offer, because I know you are sending people to me who are wise and have my best interest at heart, which is your will. I thank you Lord for removing any persons or things from my life that have been or could be a further hindrance. I ask you to continue to reveal to me any distractions during my process, and I will know that any person or things removed from my life during this process was because your almighty hand was on it, and you took it away. I will not look for any answers as to why, I trust you. Forgive me for the people or things that I have not let go. I understand that they are unhealthy to my process and pursuit to promise. Father God, today I give you a fresh Yes. I will pursue my purpose starting now without looking back. I will be strong and courageous and press forward in the things you have for me. I will praise you and glorify you in my process and pursuit to purpose.

In Jesus name I pray, Amen.

_____

_____

_____

_____

_____

_____

_____

_____

_____

_____

_____

_____

_____

_____

_____

_____

_____

_____

_____

_____

_____

_____

_____

_____

_____

_____

_____

_____

_____

_____

_____

_____

_____

_____

_____

_____

_____

_____

_____

_____

_____

_____

_____

_____

_____

_____

_____

_____

_____

_____

_____

_____

_____

_____

_____

_____

_____

_____

_____

_____

_____

_____

_____

_____

_____

_____

_____

_____

_____

_____

_____

_____

_____

_____

_____

_____

_____

_____

_____

_____

_____

Salome Williams

CHAPTER 2
WHAT HAS GOD ORDAINED
FOR YOU?

Jeremiah 1: 5
Before I formed you in your mother's womb, I knew
thee; and before you came forth out of the womb, I
sanctified thee, and I ordained you a prophet unto
these nations.

There is a purpose in you from before you were even born. This purpose is for you and generations to come. You are not on earth to just exist; you need to live. Living is using what you have for what you need and multiplying it for others. There is a work for you to do here on earth.

After God created the earth from nothing, he placed man on it. He said to Adam,

Genesis 1 vs 28
"And God blessed them, and God said, be fruitful, and
multiply, and replenish the earth, and subdue it: and
have dominion over the fish of the sea and the fowl of
the air, and over every living thing that moved upon
the earth."

My key verse for you is Genesis 1 vs 29;

²⁹ And God said, I have given you every herb bearing seed, which is upon the face of all the earth, and every tree, in which is the fruit tree of yielding seed; to which is shall be for a meat.

God has given you a seed. What will you do with that seed? Will you plant it, or will you waste it? The seed is yours to plant and multiply. Generations are dependent upon your seed.

> ### There is a seed within your seed.

I remember growing up as a little girl, I often felt out of place. Out of all my cousins and friends, I was one of the tallest and skinniest and I was a little shy.

One Christmas Eve night, my mom, dad, brother, sister, and I went out. We sat within a few feet of this huge Christmas tree in the center of the town. I was always so fascinated with the lights; I would just stare at the lights, but I would never say anything.

As I got older and started going to school, I became one of the kids that other children chose to pick on. whenever someone tried make fun of me, my younger brother would always have to fight for me.

I knew I was different, but I guess others saw me as being weird. I never tried to fit in. As a matter of a fact, I would seek to be different even if it was weird to everyone else. I am not sure why I would be so quiet, even when everyone else around me was excited about different things. I felt like I was in a box, a tall box at that. My family would say I was special, I felt loved, but just felt different.

For a long time growing up, I felt like an underdog, and now in my adult life I look out for people who currently feel the way I did. I consider myself an *Underdog Advocate.*

I know, even though I might have been overlooked, miscalculated, and looked down by many, God has a plan, and will pull on my pain to release purpose.

God has a purpose for your weakness. If you will surrender and not push to *fit in*, you will be allowing God to lead you through the process of being rejected to your destiny. By allowing purpose to be birth in me, I learn that God does not call the qualified, He qualifies those who He calls.

So, whether you have been shut up by someone else, or encountered a situation that took your voice, God will open you up for others, because there is something in you that needs to come out.

MY PRAYER FOR YOU

Father God, we worship you and praise you. You are Elohim Adoni. You are our creator, and I am blessed that you had us in mind at the ordination of creation. Lord I thank you for the life and purpose of your sons and daughters. You have established their place in the Kingdom before we knew the Light of the world. I pray your children step faithfully in the plan that you have for their life. I pray the seed of purpose begins to open and take root in their lives. I pray they rise to their highest potential. You have called them to greatness on the behalf of another, and I pray they take courage in Christ Jesus and move in confidence of who you have called them to be.

In Jesus name I pray, Amen.

WHAT HAS GOD ORDAINED FOR YOU?

Below are questions to answer regarding, What has God ordained for you? Use the pages at the end of this chapter or a separate journal to record and reflect on your answers, as you journey through your process.

1. What is the seed planted in you? What do you believe God has called you to become?
2. Have you ever felt as if you did not belong, and if so explain?
3. What are some of the doubts you have had regarding moving towards purpose?
4. What is your area(s) of weakness that would delay or prevent you from moving forward?
5. What is your painful experience that would cause you to think you were unusable by God?

YOUR PRAYER FOR PURPOSE

Elohim, I am grateful that you created me fearfully and wonderfully. There are times when I don't feel like I fit in this world, but that is because if I have your spirit within me and I am no longer of this world. I thank you that I am chosen as one of your peculiar people. I am certain that although the world may have overlooked me, I am a part of your plan and you have called me to be a deliverer for a nation of people. I am an advocate for the Kingdom of God. I know you are using my past pain for good and as I endure like a good soldier in Christ, you will bless my obedience. You are Jehovah Jireh, and you have not called me to want. I know you will send provision for me and what you have a called me to do so long as I focus on You and your Word. I pray I continuously decrease so you may increase in my life. I acknowledge my weaknesses and rely solely on you and your strength. Father I pray and yield to the call on my life,

In Jesus name, Amen.

_____

_____

_____

_____

_____

_____

_____

_____

_____

_____

_____

_____

_____

_____

_____

_____

_____

_____

_____

_____

_____

_____

_____

_____

_____

_____

CHAPTER 3
WHAT WILL IT TAKE FOR YOU
TO BIRTH IT?

Time waits on no man. If you have been given a seed and you have not planted it, what are you waiting on?

Ecclesiastes 11 vs 4 (KJV) says,
He that observes the wind shall not sow, and he that regards the clouds will not reap.

There comes a time in your life that you must *take the bull by the horn* and do what your heart is pushing you to do. Where you're from and the things you have done are not excuses for what you do and don't want to go. Use your life situations as steps on a ladder. Climb on them to reach for your attainable goals. Do not allow these things to hinder you from perusing what is truly your destiny.

When I was about 15 years old, my former Pastor spoke to me and said he would like me to conduct a service.

I said to him, "Are you sure?"

I got excited in my spirit, because I knew from Sunday school, I always wanted to do this in church. At the time, I thought moderating a service would be the coolest thing.

However, my answer to him was, "I would like to preach instead."

He seemed surprised, but to be honest, I was more surprised that I actually said that to him. Without hesitation he said, "I hope you're serious, because I am giving you that chance."

The following week I was at home preaching to the dresser and everything on it. I couldn't stop. It was as though I had been doing this every day. My dad asked me what I was doing, and I told him, practicing my sermon. I remember seeing him walking out of the room and smiling. I asked him if he would come to church to see me preach, and he said yes. I was very happy.

On the Sunday of my sermon, I became very nervous. The message was taken from St. John 4 vs 29, with the theme, "Come See a Man." I was surprised that God used such a misfit person, a weird person, in such an awesome way. I remember doing the altar call and having so many people come up for prayer. I praised God for that experience. I remember from that point on, I knew what I wanted to do, Evangelism.

Sometimes it truly takes someone else to see what's in you. It was important for my pastor to cultivate that environment, which gave me an opportunity; although at one point, I believed I did not have a voice, because of how I felt growing up. *But God*, saw me and had a plan for my life.

Don't lose hope if others don't see you and what God has truly planted on the inside of you. Once you are aware of your gift, seek God and pursue it. The support will come afterwards. There are those who will stifle you, but surround yourself with visionary people and leaders who will take a chance on you, even if it means holding you by your hand and helping you along the way.

I stayed close to my mom and one another lady who was an evangelist. I would see them go and talked with people in the community. My mom would seek out the opportunity to speak with people, just so she could talk to them about God and invite them to church.

I dreamt about purpose then, even as I do today. I would normally wake my mom and tell her about my dreams. She was a very good listener. I knew at that age I wanted to do ministry. I wanted people to know about God through the telling of the gospel and the life I lived. My goal is to always be an example for the Kingdom.

God had given me a highlight of what my purpose was, even though I knew within myself I wasn't ready for that type of responsibility at such an early age. I knew that God was calling me to something bigger than myself, and something full of purpose.

One event that had a traumatic effect on me, was the day my mother and I witnessed to two young men. I can still remember this day so clearly. We invited the men to church, and one of the young men said to me, "I'm coming to church."

The other guy responded, "When I am ready."

Not long after that encounter, we heard that they both got in an accident and one passed away.

This changed my life immensely. I cried and cried to God, "Why would you allow that to happen? Would this have happened if we had left them alone?"

I was distraught. I couldn't sleep or eat for days. At that point, evangelizing was not for me. I couldn't take on that responsibility. I ran from the presence of God after my teenage years, but God's word was always tugging on my heart.

> *Sometimes it will just take one person to help you to pull on your purpose.*

<u>What is your environment like?</u>
<u>Is it conducive for birthing your purpose?</u>

It is important to have the proper perspective when you assess your environment. Many of us were not born in luxury, and a majority did not experience the *luxury* of having a two-parent home. Perhaps where you came from was not the best place conducive to daily living; for example, growing up poor, the living situations that was not the best, experiencing financial hardship, and moving from home to home and always starting over. In severe cases, some may come from an abusive environment.

Also, for those of us who felt as if they were less than and were not "cool," feeling like an underdog, and always trying to please everyone to win.

Regardless of the pressures of your environment, purpose has to be birthed. Let me draw your attention to the story of Jesus's birth.

Luke 2 vs 7 (KJV)
"And they wrapped him in a swaddling clothes and laid Him in manger; because there was no room in the inn."

33

Baby Jesus was born in manger. Keep in mind that a manger is typically occupied by different animals, and contaminated by the animals' dung, not to mention the unknown insects that may dwell there as well. Yet, Regardless of His birthplace, Jesus was, and is today, our King of kings and Lord of lords. Our great God!

Many rejected him and turned their backs on him. He moved around and was not welcome to abide in most places. People mocked him and called him all kind of names. Many looked down on him as though he was nothing.

Maybe, just maybe, consider where you grew up, your physical and emotional environment, and all that you have had to go through was just a part of the process for greatness? Maybe, just maybe, all the things you went through were just building you for what was truly the plan of God all along.

Do not allow your environment, and what you went through, to prevent you from birthing your process. Think of it as part of God's ultimate plan for God to prosper you and see your purpose come to fruition. Sometimes there's just no room at the inn. So, let's create a room, even if it's in a manger.

Pain to Purpose

A few years after being away from God's presence and going through the process after being disobedient, heartbroken, physically abused, and homeless, I realize my environment was not conducive for purpose.

When you are out of the Will of God, you will not see your purpose; however, finding your way back to the will of the Father is an important step towards reconnecting and renewing your relationship with God. According to Psalm 51 vs 17 a broken and a contrite heart, God will not refuse.

Psalm 51 vs 17 (KJV)
The sacrifices of God are a broken spirit: a broken and a contrite heart, O God, thou wilt not despise.

And once again my soul was apprehended.

> *I realized I couldn't run*
> *For too long.*
> *God had a plan for me.*

During my process to reclaiming my position back in the Kingdom of God, I met my husband, Alrick Williams. I fell in love with him at first sight. He was the fresh breath of air that I needed. I decided the time was now, and I promised God that I will would refocus on purpose, which was always tugging on my heart.

My dad was ok with my choice to be married as long as it wasn't with someone he chased away from me in the past; however, my mom had other plans for me. She took it upon herself to speak with my husband, who was not my husband at the time. My mom didn't think this was my time, but after talking to my now husband, about what I would say, he charmed her, and she gave us her blessing.

My mom would always say, "You should be with someone who is equally yoked".

I told her, "We will be yoked. I will do everything to lead him to Christ."

Praise God, my husband is saved.

Throughout my process, in all the small and big moments, God has always been silently loud in every area of my life. I always try to see God's strength and continuously be moved by His power.

After going back to church, I realized my mind was still thinking about what traumatized me and kept me away from church. I was at our youth convention and it was time for altar call. This young girl came up to me and asked me to pray with her at the altar. I began to tremble. I was so nervous, but I knew I could not tell her no. She grabbed my hand before I said anything and we both went to the altar.

I asked her, "Why do you want to go to the altar, and why do you want

me to pray for you?"

She said, "Because, God told me so."

I knew right there and then; God had apprehended me *again* for this cause. Once again, my purpose was being revealed to me.

This thing had gotten ahold of me and it won't leave me alone.

I started to pray and weep before God, even before I began to pray for this young girl. I knew I had gone astray and left what God has called me to do, for so long. God reminded me everything I encountered and went through was a part of my process.

That night, she received the baptism of the Holy Ghost.
I was free. I knew it and I felt it. And as young as that girl was, she became a friend of mine, and is still so today. I still mentor her, and she is strong in her faith and has been working in the ministry that God has called her to.

> ## God gave me another chance.

MY PRAYER FOR YOU

Father God, I thank you that you are a God of second chances. I praise your name on high. Father I stand before you on behalf of your sons and daughters and I petition a second attempt in their lives to purpose. Your plans for them were established before creation, and they may have denied the call on their life, or denied the call because of past trauma, but I ask that the fault be cancelled in Jesus name. I pray your hand on the revelation of their call and that it becomes undeniable in this season of pursuit. For those who have not been able to firmly understand their call, I pray you send your ministering angels to them, sealing their instruction in their ear as they sleep, and your Holy Spirit be sent to quicken their spirit so the call on their life is irrefutable. Lord I pray the purpose of every hardship and disappointment be revealed for its true purpose of their process. I pray for their clarity and understanding in Jesus name,

Amen.

WHAT WILL IT TAKE FOR YOU TO BIRTH IT?

Below are questions to answer regarding, What will it take for you to birth it? Use the pages at the end of this chapter or a separate journal to record and reflect on your answers, as you journey through your process.

1. Describe a moment when God apprehended you and revealed your purpose to you.
2. Do you feel God tugging on your heart regarding moving further into your process for purpose?
3. Have you had an opportunity to experience a glimpse of what the call on your life looks like? If so, explain the experience and how you felt?
4. Have you been or felt out of the will of God, where you have not or no longer hear from God regarding your purpose?
5. If you previously knew your purpose and fell off the course to pursuing it, what brought you back to this moment, to follow through with it now?

YOUR PRAYER FOR PURPOSE

Jehovah Shammah, I thank you for your presence and the comfort of knowing that You are always there. I thank you that you have not forgotten me, even when I have forgotten myself. I thank you that you have renewed and restored your purpose in me. I thank you that you have pulled on my heart and apprehended my soul. I repent for running away from you. I repent for any actions on my behalf that led me away from your will. I know you will take what was meant to harm me and use it for my good. Because of the strength and the love of Jesus, I will not be paralyzed by fear of past experiences. I pray for a fresh anointing on my call. My faith is in you Lord, Jesus. Show me your plan and strategy for my process and what it will take to birth my purpose.

In Jesus Name I pray, Amen.

_____

_____

_____

_____

_____

_____

_____

_____

_____

_____

_____

_____

_____

_____

_____

_____

_____

_____

_____

_____

_____

_____

_____

CHAPTER 4
UNDERSTANDING PURPOSE

Hosea 4:6 (NKJV)
My people are destroyed for lack of knowledge:
because thou hast rejected knowledge, I will also reject
thee, that thou hast forgotten the law of thy God, I
will also forget thy children

What is the key to understanding what is inside of us?
First, we must know who we are.

1 Peter 2 vs 9 (KJV)
You are a chosen generation, a royal priesthood, a
holy nation, a peculiar people; that you should show
forth the praises of him who hath called you out of
darkness into his marvelous light.

God wishes for all of us to come to the knowledge and the essence of who He truly is.

> **God has entrusted**
> **Purpose within me.**

Every one of us is unique; therefore, our talents, gifts, and desires will be different. It is important to pay attention to the understanding of your purpose. Recognize it is God who has entrusted this *in* you and *with* you. Do not covet what someone else has because it looks different from yours. Perhaps in your eyes, you think their purpose is better than yours, but know where you are and be strategic in this stage of your process. It is important to take the time to plan and figure out the right steps to take.

Proverbs 14:12 (KJV)

There is a way that seems right unto a man, but the end thereof is always death.

God always looks for us to be in a state of humility and obedience, when trying to understand His purpose for our lives.

Where are we headed?

God wants to help you fulfil the purpose that is growing on the inside of you. When you are obedient to God, He will point you in the right direction. Walking in the way of the Lord does not mean things will always go smoothly; rather, it means that wherever we go, and whatever we do, we can trust God in the process to take us to the other side.

Before He formed you, He predestinated some things in your life. It's time to walk in it.

Jeremiah 29 vs 10-11

For thus saith the Lord, that after seventy years be accomplished at Babylon I will visit you, and perform my god work toward you, in causing you to return to this place. For I know the thoughts I think toward you saith the Lord, thoughts of peace, and not of evil, to give you an expected end.

Through the Lens
of the Process in Pregnancy

Perhaps you've been praying for a long time and asking God to bless your womb with a child, and you started to believe God has not seen you, and He has totally forgotten about you. In the midst of being faithful and true to Him, you feel like He has truly turned His back on you. You have everything, and the one thing that you request of Him, you are lacking and longing for.

Has God truly seen me?

Imaging one morning you get up, after waiting for such a long time to experience motherhood, your body is not feeling as usual and you are wondering if you could be pregnant.

Then, the thought comes to you, "I might be pregnant!"

You may not have uttered a word to anyone, but deep down there is an unusual feeling that points to the fact that something else is happening to your body that has never happened before. Because you are not sure, you keep quiet. Perhaps, you're not wanting to speak it prematurely, and it becomes a false alarm. This may be due to experiencing such disappointment so many times before. So, you are just not quite sure.

All you can do at this point is talk to God. "Lord, is this true? Can this truly be? "Might I be pregnant?"

All throughout the day you have the urge to go and purchase a pregnancy test. After hours of contemplating, you finally go and buy the test.

After testing, while being suspicious and surprised, you learn you are pregnant. At first, you are excited, but there is still some doubt in your mind.

"Could it really be?" You say to the Lord, "I have been doubting you all this time, now you have proven yourself to me. You have answered my prayer."

This brings me to Mary, The mother of Jesus.

Luke 1 vs 34

"How will this be," Mary asked the angel, "since I am a virgin?" "The Holy Spirit will come on you, and the power of the Most High will overshadow you. So the holy one to be born will be called the Son of God.

Do not doubt what God has given you.

Once you realize this possible pregnancy may be a reality, you took another pregnancy test. With the positive result you screamed on top of your lungs, "Oh my God, I am truly pregnant!"

This news took you over the moon and back, you couldn't wait to tell everyone including your spouse.

Now that you are sure of what you are carrying, all the mental planning begins.

You have been asking God to reveal Himself to you and now He has. Now He has truly seen you.

Beer-Lahai-Roi – "The well of him that liveth and seeth me"

MY PRAYER FOR YOU

Father God, You are Alpha and Omega, the beginning and the end. You are the all-knowing God, El Shaddai almighty. I am grateful for the purpose you have planted in your children. Thank you, Father, that you have given the desire of the heart to your children who delight in you. I pray that they know who they are, and Who's they are. We belong to a good – good, God, and Father. You give the best gifts. I pray the spirit of lack off your children, in Jesus name, and I loose your abundance and favor over them. I pray that their minds be equipped with the knowledge of their sonship, through the love of Christ Jesus. Father I place spiritual hands on the womb of ever reader, and I breath life over the seed in their womb. May they rejoice in the Lord for the assurance that today is the day their process has purpose.

In Jesus name I pray, Amen.

UNDERSTANDING PURPOSE

Below are questions to answer regarding, Understanding Purpose. Use the pages at the end of this chapter or a separate journal to record and reflect on your answers, as you journey through your process.

1. Have you ever looked at someone's situation and wished it was yours? If so, explain what it was that you saw, that made you feel you were missing out?

2. What is something you have believed God for, but it has not happened? What desire do you have in your heart that has not come to pass?

3. Is it possible you have been pregnant, but have not began nurturing what it is that God has placed in you, because you have doubted your ability to carry it?

YOUR PRAYER FOR PURPOSE

Lord God, how excellent is your name in all the earth. I thank you Lord, that you are a covenant keeping God. You have established purpose in me and have called me to be fruitful and multiply. I ask your forgiveness for not walking in covenant with you and delaying my process. I repent for any coveting thoughts of wanting what my neighbor has, instead of seeking out the best you have for me. I thank you that you have planted seed in my womb. I am grateful that the doubt has been washed away and replaced with courage. I call out to my Lord, Jehovah Nissi, and I take courage to produce and become all that God almighty has called me to be. I am anxious for nothing, and I know by prayer, supplication, and thankfulness, Jehovah has gone ahead of me to prepare the way. The battles in my process to purpose has already been won.

In Jesus Name I pray, Amen.

CHAPTER 5
THE MENTAL PROCESS

"Will it be a boy or a girl?"

"What shall I name the baby?"

"What do I do now?"

"How will I decorate the room?"

"Should start shopping now."

"How am I going to share this with my husband?"

Once you accept the fact that you are pregnant, all of these different thoughts, coupled with emotions, begins to go off in your mind.

Continuing to image you are pregnant, every morning you wake up and the first thing you begin to do is thank God for blessing you with this baby. You rub on your belly, while looking in the mirror to see if your tummy has started to show. You are so filled with joy; you just want to shout it on the mountain top.

When God has placed something on the inside of you, or into your hands, you have to understand that the end result is dependent on not only your initial reaction, but your initial mental state, and the careful planning of how to handle things at each and every stage of the process.

Overjoyed and grateful that God has finally answered your prayers, your secret is uncontainable. You are pushed to share the great news and now you are eagerly excited to share it, but first with your spouse. You know your husband would be thoroughly excited, because it has been such a long time waiting, and now you both can finally celebrate and enjoy parenthood, even though it's quite early in the process.

Sharing your dreams and purpose in this early stage, and with the right people, is also crucial in this process. There are dream killers, purpose killers, and destiny killers. There are those that would rather see you stuck than trying to excel; however, it is very important to keep a positive mindset.

John 10 vs 10 says:
The thief does not come except to steal, and to kill, and to destroy. I have come that they may have life, and that they may have it more abundantly.

I believe Mary was comforted when she found out that Elizabeth was also pregnant. They both were happy for each other.

Luke 1 vs 41
And it came to pass that when Elisabeth heard the salutation of Mary, the baby leaped in her womb; and Elisabeth was filled with the Holy Ghost.

It is such a wonderful thing to be associated with people that will be happy for you, your gift, your blessings, and your purpose. It doesn't matter how old you are. It doesn't matter how young you are. It's never too late or too early for your purpose to come alive.

MY PRAYER FOR YOU

Father God, I thank you for your tender hand on your children during this time of preparation for purpose. You have shown yourself to be a promise keeper and have given us seed in the ground. Father I pray that your children stay in faith and rely on your Word for guidance in all decisions that are to be made during their process. I pray for right alignments and sound judgement in their journey.

In Jesus name I pray, Amen.

THE MENTAL PROCESS

Below are questions to answer regarding, The Mental Process. Use the pages at the end of this chapter or a separate journal to record and reflect on your answers, as you journey through your process.

1. What are some of the fears that have tried to take over your mind, as you have accepted the idea of giving birth to purpose?

2. Have you been emotional during your process to purpose? If so, explain which emotions you have had to overcome.

3. What type of company do you keep? Are you surrounded by people who encourage you or discourage you?

4. Have you identified any toxic people who you need to remove from your life during this season?

5. Do you have someone who is aware of the desires of your heart, who is in agreement with you in prayer over the life of this desire? If so who, and if not, who do you believe God has sent to you as a partner or midwife in this process?

YOUR PRAYER FOR PURPOSE

Jehovah Shalom, I am thankful for your Spirit of Peace in my mind and throughout my life. I am praying for your peace in every area of my decision making. I pray for the gift of discerning spirits, that I may be able to understand what is in operation within those around me. I pray against being double minded and repent for any indecisiveness that I have acted in. I know a double minded man is wicked in all his ways, so I ask for the mind of Christ. You have not given us a spirit of fear, but of power, love, and a sound mind. I thank you Lord for sending likeminded people to walk alongside my process. I pray for Godly connections, and I cancel the assignment of any unholy covenants that have been made. I pray anyone with false intentions to sabotage my process to purpose be exposed and removed by the hand of God.

In Jesus Name I pray, Amen.

_____

_____

_____

_____

_____

_____

_____

_____

_____

_____

_____

_____

_____

_____

_____

_____

_____

_____

_____

_____

_____

_____

_____

_____

_____

_____

_____

_____

CHAPTER 6
THE WAITING

Psalm 27 vs 14

Wait on the LORD: be of good courage, and he shall strengthen thine heart: wait, I say, on the LORD.

The process will cost more than the purpose, the gift, or the destiny. Even waiting in the process isn't easy, but necessary. Everything will not happen right away, especially without some obstacles thrown in the midst of waiting. This is to test your faith in God throughout the process.

It is important for you to pray and wait upon God. Not just praying when things come upon you, but have a prayerful life and an intimate relationship with God that will sustain you as you wait on Him.

Daniel prayed and waited upon God. God spoke to him in the time when it felt as though he was in complete darkness. Often times, this is how and when God shows up.

Throughout the early stages of pregnancy, anxiety will flare up. It is important to strategize your pregnancy process for the upcoming days and months. But, although you are planning in your process of pregnancy, you will need to take some time to pause and just breathe. Everything will not happen at once. Take one day at a time. The same God who blesses you, will carry you through.

We need to be able to connect with God and know that even if He does not come right away, believe that He will. There is a saying that goes,

"He may not come when you want him, but he is always on time."

I realize it is when our situations are at the roughest point of the process, that God shows up. When you're at your darkest time, God will strengthen you. The time when we want to give up, and when the pressure seems unbearable, is when it's time for your exit.

When we pray and wait upon God, He will never let us down.
In Daniel 3 vs 18, Shadrack, Meshach and Abednego said, "Even if God does not deliver us, we will not bow."

Can we truly say this when we are in the heat of our battles?

During this waiting period or pregnancy, you are faced with all kinds of ill feelings and may not be able to keep anything down in your stomach. You may become nauseous and have feelings of wanting to projectile. This is when your ecstatic feelings of pregnancy seem to be overshadowed by the way you're feeling in this stage of your process.

Don't allow the things that are around you to overwhelm you, especially when your purpose is being enlightened as you go through the different phases.

Wait on the Lord and be of good courage and he will strengthen you.

Joshua 1 vs 9
Have I not commanded you? Be strong and courageous.
Do not be afraid; do not be discouraged, for the LORD
your God will be with you wherever you go."

Pray and be Patient

Understand this, when you have become overwhelmed, even with what you have prayed and asked God for, it affects you, not only spiritually, but psychologically, and physiologically. It will take you to a place of isolation. Food may not even be important. However, you need to feed that baby in order for the baby to grow healthy and for you to remain strong. The health of your baby is dependent of how you eat.

The purpose that has been given and highlighted in you, needs to be fed with positive thoughts, true dedication, and the right people in your life. Be careful how you are fed when you're empty and be careful of who speaks into your life. The word of God must be spoken over your dreams, over your purpose, over your destiny, and over your fertile ground. It is important for you to know, that in order for your purpose to grow, you must keep being fed with the Word of God.

MY PRAYER FOR YOU

Father God, I am thankful for who and what you are. You are Omniscient. I thank you that you give rest to your children as you have gone ahead to prepare the way for them. You know what lies ahead of them in their process, and you remain faithful and true to your Word. I thank you Father for your light in the moments of their journey when the road appears dark, we know that you are working on their behalf to fool the enemy.

In Jesus name I pray, Amen.

THE WAITING

Below are questions to answer regarding, The Waiting. Use the pages at the end of this chapter or a separate journal to record and reflect on your answers, as you journey through your process.

1. Have you had thoughts of giving up in your process? If so, explain.
2. Do you struggle with patience? If so, explain your difficulties and any strategy to improve.
3. Have you made any changes in your physical life to adjust to your process? If you have not, consider what changes you now feel may be beneficial to your process.
4. What are some of your go to scriptures to increase your faith when you are waiting on the Lord?

YOUR PRAYER FOR PURPOSE

Father God, I thank you for your fruit of the Spirit Patience. I know that patience is key to my process. Patience is a must to endure. Patience is also my key to resting in faith. I know that you are working on my behalf. I thank you that you are making a way for me. I will be still and know that you are God almighty. I will praise you and worship your name in the process, because you are worthy to be praised. I ask for your grace in this season as I change my habits and remove the things I rely on as comfort, but may be unhealthy to my process. I don't mind waiting on you Lord. I thank you for trusting me with this seed of purpose, and I will endure the process.

In Jesus name I pray, Amen.

_____

_____

_____

_____

_____

_____

_____

_____

_____

_____

_____

_____

_____

_____

_____

_____

_____

_____

_____

_____

_____

_____

_____

_____

_____

_____

_____

_____

_____

_____

_____

_____

_____

_____

_____

_____

_____

_____

_____

_____

_____

_____

_____

_____

_____

_____

_____

_____

_____

_____

_____

_____

_____

_____

_____

_____

CHAPTER 7
GROWING SPIRITUALLY
IN THE PROCESS

I realize that I found myself growing spiritually in the process. The bible says,

Romans 5 vs 2-4

By whom also we have access through faith into this grace wherein we stand, and rejoice in hope of the glory of God. And not only so, but we glory in tribulations: also knowing that tribulation worketh patience; and patience, experience; and experience and hope. And hope makes not ashamed.

Exercising faith in the process will grow your faith in God. I recognize when I ask God for patience, He will allow somethings to try my patience. In the beginning, I would normally fail, but then the next time I am alert, because He allows my mind to remember this is what I asked for. This is the way it will be shown, through experience.

If you are disciplined enough and consistent enough, sooner than later you will be able to lift that desired amount of weight to take you to the next level in your process. Likewise, with your faith; if you exercise it long enough, you will be amazed how far you can go, how much you would grow, and how many obstacles you will be able to overcome. Recognizing the same God who gave you purpose and helped you in the early stage of the process, is the same God that is with you always.

Isaiah 41:10

Fear not, for I am with thee: be not dismayed for I am thy God: I will strengthen thee. I will uphold thee with the right hand of my righteousness.

So it is, when we set a spiritual goal for ourselves, the purpose within us must be fulfilled. There is a requirement and a process that we have to go through.

Athletes who lift weights starts with the minimal amount they can lift. But the consistency of lifting small amount will cause you to be able to add more over a period of time.

There are some things attached to your purpose that require growth. There are some hiccups during this trimestral process. During this time, you have to pace yourself and take it easy, you don't want to lose this pregnancy, because you were too busy doing this and that and trying to get everything done all at once.

You can rest and still find time to get in your secret place to ask God for help in the next stage of the process.

Seek God for strategies to cope during this process as you wait for this season to pass

MY PRAYER FOR YOU

Heavenly Father, hallowed be they name. I give you the glory, the honor, and the praise. I thank you for your Word. Without your Word, we would not know the truth of who you are and how you love us. I pray that as your children journey through their process to birthing purpose, they increase in faith. I pray the knowledge and understanding of Christ Jesus take root in their belly, and that they are full on the bread of life. They will know that they have fullness of the Lord is within them and their faith will increase because the Word of the Lord is true and living. I thank you for the power that is given to those who believe. I pray you children increase in a new measure of father, and they find the authority of their voice, and command what needs to be moved out of they their path. I pray that ever Word of the Lord spoken over their lives is activated now, by the Spirit of the Lord.

In Jesus name I pray, Amen.

GROWING SPIRITUALLY IN THE PROCESS

Below are questions to answer regarding, Growing Spiritually in the Process. Use the pages at the end of this chapter or a separate journal to record and reflect on your answers, as you journey through your process.

1. How often do you read the Word of God? Do you feel you need to increase your time in the Word?

2. Do you feel you are too busy? Are there somethings that could be removed from your plate?

3. Are you weak in your faith? In what area do you believe you need to increase your faith.

4. Use these scriptures to meditate on to increase your faith.

- Hebrews 11:1 ESV - Now faith is the assurance of things hoped for, the conviction of things not seen.

- Romans 10:17 ESV - So faith comes from hearing, and hearing through the word of Christ.

- Matthew 21:22 ESV - And whatever you ask in prayer, you will receive, if you have faith.

- Mark 11:22-24 ESV - And Jesus answered them, "Have faith in God. Truly, I say to you, whoever says to this mountain, 'Be taken up and thrown into the sea,' and does not doubt in his heart, but believes that what he says will come to pass, it will be done for him. Therefore I tell you, whatever you ask in prayer, believe that you have received it, and it will be yours.

- 1 Corinthians 2:5 ESV - That your faith might not rest in the wisdom of men but in the power of God.

- Ephesians 2:8-9 ESV - For by grace you have been saved through faith. And this is not your own doing; it is the gift of God, not a result of works, so that no one may boast.

- Luke 1:37 ESV - For nothing will be impossible with God.

- Proverbs 3:5-6 ESV - Trust in the Lord with all your heart, and do not lean on your own understanding. In all your ways acknowledge him, and he will make straight your paths.

- 2 Corinthians 5:7 ESV - For we walk by faith, not by sight.

- Hebrews 11:6 ESV - And without faith it is impossible to please him, for whoever would draw near to God must believe that he exists and that he rewards those who seek him.

- 2 Timothy 4:7 ESV - I have fought the good fight, I have finished the race, I have kept the faith.

- Galatians 2:20 ESV - I have been crucified with Christ. It is no longer I who live, but Christ who lives in me. And the life I now live in the flesh I live by faith in the Son of God, who loved me and gave himself for me.

YOUR PRAYER FOR PURPOSE

Father God, I thank you for your presence in my life, and that you made a way for me to know you as my Father, Lord Jesus, and the Holy Spirit. Father I ask your forgiveness for the moments I have not relied on the faith you have given me. I ask for forgiveness for not being dedicated to the study of your Word to the decree that you have called me to be. I believe what you have called me to become is possible. It is not me, but you who will be moving on my behalf. I will walk by faith in this process. I am faithful that you will shape my purpose. I will believe what you have told me. I will believe it until I see it. I am in agreement with your Word. You know the plan that you had for me and I will do my part by staying in your Word to growing spiritually in the process. I believe the plan on my life and am faithful you will reveal the strategy.

In Jesus name I pray, Amen.

_____

_____

_____

_____

_____

_____

_____

_____

_____

_____

_____

_____

_____

_____

_____

_____

_____

_____

_____

_____

_____

_____

_____

_____

_____

_____

_____

_____

_____

_____

_____

_____

_____

_____

_____

_____

_____

_____

_____

_____

_____

_____

_____

_____

_____

_____

_____

_____

_____

_____

_____

_____

_____

_____

_____

CHAPTER 8
EXPANDING IN YOUR PROCESS

At this stage, your purpose will be expanding for others to see.

Luke 1 vs 64

64 And his mouth was opened immediately, and his tongue loosed, and he spoke, and praised God.

65 And fear came on all that dwelt round about them: and all these sayings were noised abroad throughout all the hill country of Judaea.

66 And all they that heard them laid them up in their hearts, saying, what manner of child this shall be! And the hand of the Lord was with him.

During this expansion time, people will begin to see what God has blessed you with, your purpose will begin to show and shift somethings around you.

1 Chronicles 4vs 9-10

And Jabez called on the God of Israel, saying, Oh that thou wouldest bless me indeed, and enlarge my coast, and that thine hand might be with me, and that thou wouldest keep me from evil, that it may not grieve me! And God granted him that which he requested.

When you are expanding, you will start to see who is for or against you. It is imperative for you to be spiritually aware of who you allow to be part of what God has called you into. Spiritual discernment is necessary. You will need a team who will help cheer you on and offer support to you during this time. You will need someone, but you will not need everyone.

Note, when you are being expanded, your capacity for understanding will increase. Elevation brings revelation. As God elevates you in your purpose, it will surely make sense why you really had to go through the process. The higher you go, the more you see, and the clearer things will appear. Keep the faith, because generations will be positively affected by your vision.

There will be a great manifestation on you that will change the trajectory of your life and the people around you. Generations will be birthed, and legacy will be formed, because you are on the process to purpose.

After I went back to church, I realized, in my mind, I was still thinking about what had traumatized me and kept me away from church. And so, I had to pray and ask God to help me block out the thoughts. I realized, the more I sought after God and grew in Him, the clearer things became to me.

As the knowledge of God began to expand in my comprehension, I recognized the confusion caused by the devil; he worked through people that were close to me and used them to distract and discouraged me. I can't say it didn't get to me. Sometimes, it made me cry, but when remembered where God has brought me from, and where I am today, or when I think of the fact that I don't look like what I've been through, and today I am not who I use to be or where I was coming from, it gives me courage to fight and go on.

There will be times on your journey, or in your process, you feel like there is more against you than for you. Just know, it is only devil playing tricks on you. Greater is He that is in you, than he that is in the world.

Isiah 57 vs 14

No weapon that rise up against me shall prosper and every tongue that shall rise against me shall be condemn.

Salome Williams

MY PRAYER FOR YOU

Father God, I thank you for being a Father who gives good gifts to His children. You have offered your children the access to spiritual gifts if they desire them, and I thank you for the access to spiritual discernment. I pray that your sons and daughter's capacity for spiritual understanding expands. Their capacity for the love of the Word increases, I pray their capacity for seeing You in all that they do is enlarged. I pray their focus and eyes are set on Christ Jesus, and they discover Him in all that they do and experience.

In Jesus name I pray, Amen.

EXPANDING IN YOUR PROCESS

Below are questions to answer regarding, Expanding in Your Process.
Use the pages at the end of this chapter or a separate journal to record
and reflect on your answers, as you journey through your process.

1. What are the negative thoughts that continue to consume you?
2. What battles do you normally come up against?
3. Things are often more than what they seem. Tapping into your spiritual discernment, what do you believe God is showing you, or how do you believe God is using what is meant for your harm, for good?

YOUR PRAYER FOR PURPOSE

Father God, I thank you for the assurance in knowing that all that I go through, I know you have given me a spirit of Power to stand strong and overcome all that I face. I know you fight my battles and the power I possess is to stay steadfast in you. I thank you for the spirit of Love. Because I have the mind of Christ and the heart of God, and I am able to see past any hurt or distractions, that the enemy may have tried to use against me by using those around me, because I know I don't fight against flesh and blood. I thank you father for a sound mind. I am able to access and use your knowledge and wisdom in my process. I cast down every thought and imagination that has tried to delay my process or move me off the path to birth my promise. I know my promise is of God and anything that challenges the truth of that promise, which is in me, has risen above the will of God. I will not be dismayed. I will be strong faithful. Thank you, Lord, for enlarging my mental capacity and my reach to others.

In Jesus name I pray, Amen.

_____

_____

_____

_____

_____

_____

_____

_____

_____

_____

_____

_____

_____

_____

_____

_____

_____

_____

_____

_____

_____

_____

_____

_____

_____

_____

_____

_____

Salome Williams

CHAPTER 9
TESTING DURING THE PROCESS

The spirit of giving up usually rises during our process to greatness. The process cost a lot in reaching your purpose. When we want certain things in life, we recognize how much work we have to put into it. If it doesn't cost you, it's not worth it.

Our testing will come in all different forms during our process.
In the growth of my marriage, God has taken us through some trying times. The fruit of the Spirit had to be evident in my marriage, especially before my husband got saved. There was a burden on me to ensure that my life was an example that would lead my husband to Christ. Thanks to the almighty God, my husband and son are both saved. Thanks to Jehovah for giving me the endurance through the different areas of my life.

Going through multiple miscarriages had been really hard for us, more so for me. I lamented to God so many times asking him, "WHY?"

I found myself pulling out my long question list of theodicies, whenever I'm in reflections of the pain of losing someone I felt so connected to, yet I didn't even get to carry to full term.

I recognize that in every area, there were different processes.

You will find out that as often as we get over one obstacle, there is always another one around the corner. Now I can testify, and let you know that God will bring you out of your situation. He never fails.

God would answer me in the little of things. He would sometimes say, *"My Child,"* and even when I couldn't understand *"My Child"*, I knew although I went through what I went through, I was still *His child.*

Through it all, God's hand is still on our lives throughout our process. I recognize if I don't have a process, there will be no manifestation of God's purpose on my life.

Throughout our lifetime, we journey through many seasons. Each season represents the continuous work that God is doing in our life. Sometimes, we have questions about what is happening, and we are not sure how to deal with it. But according to:

Ecclesiastes 3 vs 1 & 11

1To every thing there is a season, and a time to every purpose under the heaven

11 He hath made every thing beautiful in his time: also he hath set the world in their heart, so that no man can find out the work that God maketh from the beginning to the end.

In everything we go through, God knows about it and He is working it out for our good, to them that love Him and to them who are called, according to His purpose.

Use your process to give God Glory, know when it is all said and done, God is using your fight to make you a great testimony.

MY PRAYER FOR YOU

Father God, I am thankful you are faithful to keep you hand on your children as they journey through their process. I pray that your strength surrounds them during their season of testing and growth. I pray for your Spirit of Peace and Comfort to cover them. I pray that their ears are tuned in to hearing your sweet quiet voice, and that they may move quickly and swiftly as the Spirit of God leads them through this season. May they know they have the strength to endure, in Christ Jesus.

In Jesus name I pray, Amen.

TESTING DURING THE PROCESS

Below are questions to answer regarding, Testing During the Process.
Use the pages at the end of this chapter or a separate journal to record
and reflect on your answers, as you journey through your process.

1. What is a situation where you asked God, "Why?"
2. Did you pray on the situation and asked God to reveal to you what was really behind the matter? Did God reveal it to you?
3. We all have a season of testing. When is your season of testing and how does God test you?
4. Your testing leads to your testimony, what is the beginning of your story?

YOUR PRAYER FOR PURPOSE

Father God, I thank you for the unction of the Holy Spirit my life. I thank you for your hand. You have taken me by the hand and are leading me through this very uncomfortable place. I repent for any upset or anger that I may have had towards you for my trails. I understand there is purpose in everything. I have asked for this cup to pass me, but I know your will is greater. I pray that I endure this process to birthing my purpose like a good soldier in Christ Jesus. There is purpose in my testimony, and it will be used to glorify your name.

In Jesus name I pray, Amen.

_____

_____

_____

_____

_____

_____

_____

_____

_____

_____

_____

_____

_____

_____

_____

_____

_____

_____

_____

_____

_____

_____

_____

_____

_____

_____

_____

_____

_____

_____

_____

_____

_____

_____

_____

_____

_____

_____

_____

_____

_____

_____

_____

_____

_____

_____

_____

_____

_____

_____

_____

_____

_____

_____

_____

_____

CHAPTER 10
ACKNOWLEDGING WEAKNESSES IN THE PROCESS

Luke 22 vs 31

Simon, Simon, behold, Satan asked to have you, that he might sift you like wheat.

Be careful of going back to the same old habits. There are some things you must put away, now that you are pregnant. There are a number of foods and drinks you cannot ingest while being pregnant. There are also places you can no longer go.

Romans 7 vs 20-24

I find then a law, that, when I want to do good, evil is present with me.
For I delight in the law of God after the inward man
But I see another law in my members, warring against the law of my mind, and bringing me into captivity to the law of sin which is in my members.

Be careful of who's in your circle and who you associate yourself to. There are certain things we cannot allow ourselves to go back into, when we have been called into our purpose. Dissociation is necessary at this point. If it will not push you towards the expected end, distance is necessary. Anything and anyone that will prevent you from fulfilling your purpose is a weakness.

When you are pregnant, there are certain things you cannot do anymore. Especially things that will add to your weight. Unnecessary weight will immobilize you. Do not let negativity cause you to be too weighty. That is an extra load you don't want to carry with your purpose.

There is something that God has placed on the inside of you that is called PURPOSE. Purpose has weight attached to it. There is a responsibility within us, and it is placed upon us to carry, and carry well. There are people that are depending on us. We are carrying generations inside of us.

You will often feel like the weight is too much, because after a while it gets heavier and heavier. The weight will cause your back to hurt, and your feet to swell. Sometimes you may feel like you want to just stay in one place.

Recognizing our weaknesses in this process is important, because it will push us to call upon God. We will begin to understand, that even though God gave us this purpose, this destiny, and this gift, we know we truly can't carry it and fulfil it without Him.

MY PRAYER FOR YOU

Father God, I am thankful for your Word. The bible says Jesus is the Word. "In the beginning was the Word, and the Word was with God, and the Word was God (John 1:1)." I am thankful that you have given your Son to us. I thank you Father for Jehovah Shammah who is always with is on our weakness. I thank you for Jehovah Shalom with is covering us with peace. I thank you that Jesus is the Truth, who we cannot do anything against it. I am thankful that Jehovah Roi is caring for us in these times of weakness. I thank you Father that you are the one whom we can depend on at all times in our life.

In Jesus name I pray, Amen.

ACKNOWLEDGING WEAKNESSES IN THE PROCESS

Below are questions to answer regarding, Acknowledging Weakness in the Process. Use the pages at the end of this chapter or a separate journal to record and reflect on your answers, as you journey through your process.

1. What is your strongest area of weakness? This is most likely the thing that you have maintained control over and have not presented to God to take full possession of, in your life. This may be the thing you are most afraid to expose, because it is exposing this weakness to others may seem as if it disqualifies you and your process.

YOUR PRAYER FOR PURPOSE

Father God, I surrender to you this day. I make a new commitment to honor your and live by your will. I chose to live by the Word of God and desire your perfect will in my life. I release to you all that I have held on to, for comfort and security. I release this to you, because these are burdens you did not give me to bare. Today I submit myself to you and I decrease. I take a step back so that you may rise high in my life and be the strength that I require to move ahead in my process. I bind the spirit of pride that has laid hidden in my decisions and I loose the humility of the servant over my life. I ask you Father, that as I continue this process, you expose the prideful thoughts that remain in my mind. I am on a path to greatness. As I endure this valley, I follow you. I know that you would never leave me, nor forsake me. I thank you King Jesus.

In Jesus name I pray, Amen.

CHAPTER 11
STRENGTH DURING THE PROCESS

James 2 vs 1-2
Consider it pure joy, when we come into various trials, because they are immensely valuable to the strengthening of our spirituality.

There is a part of your journey where things will become hard and difficult to manage. At this point in the process you may become weaker. There will be times when you feel like giving up and want to just *throw in the towel*. It will seem as though the darkness will not leave you; the load gets heavier, the pain is more intensified, and there is a feeling of not being able to go on.

Proverbs 3 vs 5-6
Trust in the Lord with all your heart and lean not to your own understanding, but in all thy ways acknowledge Him and he shall direct your path.

Finding your strength is crucial at this stage. The word of God gives you strength from within. We meditate on it day and night. Knowing there is an expected end will encourage you to hold on and persevere. It is imperative for you to know at this stage in the process, when it looks as though the purpose is getting away from you, the situations that arise are opportunities for God to show Himself strong, in you.

> ## "The joy of the Lord is my strength."
> ## Nehemiah 8:10

Hebrew 12 vs 1-2

Therefore we also, since we are surrounded by so great a cloud of witnesses, let us lay aside every weight, and the sin which so easily ensnares us, and let us run with endurance the race that is set before us, 2 looking unto Jesus, the [a]author and [b]finisher of our faith, who for the joy that was set before Him endured the cross, despising the shame, and has sat down at the right hand of the throne of God.

The moments in your life when you have been seeking, knocking, and asking, has led you to God, who has been waiting to do and give you something that will propel you to a greatness beyond measure. When you are near purpose, you receive joy. It feels like you're on top of the world and you can shout it from the mountain top and let everyone know; especially those who have been routing for you.

The journey in fulfilling one's purpose is like a race. There is a baton to be passed, there are corners along the way, and there are many hurdles you will need to jump over to get to the finish line. Nevertheless, you are being encouraged to hold the baton, to stay in your lane, and run the race. You will never get a prize if you haven't completed your race; you will never get a certificate before you complete the course. Process leads to purpose.

2 Corinthians 2vs 12
And he said unto me, my grace is sufficient for thee:
for my strength is made perfect in your weakness.

While you are still expanding, you are feeling all the weight and the stress that is beginning to affect every area of your life. Unable to do much, you are now dependent upon outside help. You can hardly do things for yourself. This is when you are getting closer to your expected end. This is when God is ready to fulfill purpose in you and cause life to come forth. Even though it's harder than when you started, the joy of bringing forth life shines through the hard times.

Psalm 46 vs 1
God is our refuge and strength, a very present help in
trouble.

Salome Williams

MY PRAYER FOR YOU

Father God, how blessed are we that we have your unimaginable goodness and favor in our lives? I pray your favor over your sons and daughter and ask for your grace in every area of their lives. I pray for your divine influence to take over their plans and efforts, that they me rest in the Lord and know that your Grace is sufficient. There is nothing stronger that can access their lives and give the endurance required to complete their assignments. Father they are at a race for the finish line, so I pray their eyes and ears are in tuned with your voice, they are renewed daily with your supernatural divine strength to endure, that the resist temptations that will cause delay, and they embody your divine excellence in all that they do.

In Jesus name I pray, Amen.

STREGNTH DURING THE PROCESS

Below are questions to answer regarding, Strength During the Process. Use the pages at the end of this chapter or a separate journal to record and reflect on your answers, as you journey through your process.

1. Review your areas of weakness and rewrite your perspective of how you see the weakness, replacing the worry, doubt, or shame, with a joyful outcome. What are you believe for, now that you have exchanged your weakness for the strength and favor of the Lord?

YOUR PRAYER FOR PURPOSE

Father God, I thank you for the comfort of knowing you are the medicine needed to strengthen my body, soul, and spirit. I thank you for your joy. I am faithful in knowing that because of your sacrifice, the joy of the Lord is my strength. Through all hardships, heaviness, and times when I feel as though I cannot go another day, I know the truth is your love for me turns my weeping into joy and laughter. I thank you that Joy is the cure. I pray I see Jesus in everything I do, and I find the peace, love, and joy of the Lord in those precious moments. I pray that my faithfulness to the process gives you great joy. I will complete this process to purpose with faith and walking in truth. I serve you Lord, and my mission is to glorify your name through the highs and the lows of my journey. I thank you for your strength, and rejoice with a glorious, inexpressible joy.

In Jesus name I pray, Amen.

CHAPTER 12
PREPARE TO PUSH

As I study the pregnancy process a little closer, I recognize the third trimester is the most exciting stage and is the hardest part of the birthing journey. You are quite uncomfortable, and you are just ready to give birth. No sleeping position will do, and the baby is growing faster than ever.

So, you prayed for a child and God granted you your wish. You went through the different trimesters, and now you're almost at the end, but the pressure is worse than before.

Why is this so?

In this stage, your water brakes, you become fatigue, achy, you lack bladder control, etc. This is when the baby's brain is rapidly developing and is now sensitive to light and sound. Infants can now open his/her eyes and look down and out.

Ready to be born.

During this last phase is when you truly need strong support? This is the dilation and stretching period. When your purpose is getting ready to burst and produce, understand that there are many discomforts that will occur. You will have the urge to push. The process will seem slow to ending and perhaps will weary you. Remember the word that says:

Galatians 6 vs 9:
And let us not be weary in well doing; for in due season will reap if we faint not. As we have therefore opportunity, let us do well unto all.

Now that you have gone through the process, after favor, anointing, strength, etc., you are ready to push.

The pain has now awakened you, late in the midnight hour. You weren't expecting it, because your due date has not come yet; however, it's time.

Your husband says, "Honey, I need to get you to the hospital."

You respond, "Babe, I don't think I can wait."

While you're in pain and getting ready to push, he stops you by saying, "Honey, you can't give birth here. You need to go to the hospital!"

You mustered up some courage and manage to get into the car. The pain becomes so unbearable, and the ride gets bumpy as you try not to push, but you must. The paramedic is on the phone, but you can't stop the baby from crowning.

You don't want to push, but you have to.

There is no choice at this point, and all you truly have is you husband. Your husband stops the car, and with the help of the paramedics on the line, he then says to you, "Honey, this has been a process and a roller coaster ride. We prayed for this; God answered our prayers."

Even though this is not the environment conducive to having a baby, at this point, it doesn't matter. Your husband continues to follow the instructions from the paramedics on the line. He succeeds in helping you deliver the baby. He wraps up the baby up and lays him in your arms.

CHANELLING THE PURPOSE

You are chosen

You are gifted

You are pregnant with purpose

You are in waiting

You are expanding

And now, we must understand where we are in the process.

How will people be affected by your purpose?

Will it bring forth the next generation into greatness? Far surpass what you have done?

Will it inspire others to find their purpose?

Will it aide in helping others through their process to purpose?

Will it cause growth in every area of your lives, and the lives of those who are around you, even unto generations to come?

Understanding our process, will allow us to see that it is really not about the process, or about the journey, it's about the destination.

You have come thus far, now this is all you.

You are almost at the finish line.

Get ready!

Set!!

Push!!!

Push pass your pain

Push pass your discomfort

Push pass your fatigue

Push pass the waiting

Push pass the weight

Push pass the weaknesses

Push with all your strength

Push pass all your circumstances and God will carry you through

Remember it's just a process.

Giving birth to purpose in an uncomfortable place.

As you seek God for a seed, for purpose, for something that is much bigger than you, something that will impact others and affect generations, just know that God is right there with you. He wants you to know that He sees you. He knows who you are and what your heart desires. He has not forgotten about you; He has not turned his back on you.

If you are in a dry place and without hope or, perhaps your environment feels as dry as a desert, know that God is with you. He will water your dry ground, and He will cause water to spring up in the deserted area in your life. He will cause your seed to grow and bring forth in due season.

You can give birth in an uncomfortable environment.

God will lift your seed and purpose and make great nations of it. Today let God be your:

BEER-LAHAI-ROI
The well of the one who liveth and sees me

MY PRAYER FOR YOU

Father God, I pray for this reader, that they will find their strength and purpose in you. I pray that they have found the hidden jewels within this book that are key treasures to help them in their process. Father no one said it would be easy birthing the seed that you have planned within us, so I pray that your children increase in faith, understanding, and wisdom to endure their birthing season. You know what we are able to carry. I pray for your Spirit of might and grace over them to finish. This is their finish season. I pray the knowledge of knowing they can do all things through Christ Jesus who strengthens them, and you Father God, have called them to such a time as this.

In Jesus name I pray, Amen.

PREPARE TO PUSH

Below are questions to answer regarding, Prepare to Push. Use the pages at the end of this chapter or a separate journal to record and reflect on your answers, as you journey through your process.

1. What are you birthing? What has God revealed to you, that you are carrying. It is time to Claim it and Name it. Every day, remind yourself of what you are carrying and birthing, so when it is time to push, you will see the life in your purpose, and you will not quit.

YOUR PRAYER FOR PURPOSE

Father God, I thank you for Purpose. I thank you that you are trusting me with an assignment for the Kingdom. I thank you that I a have favor with you and with man. I will commit to this process and will endure until the fruit of what I carry is produced and you are glorified. I am a planter, a sower, a harvester, a finisher. I can do all things through Christ who strengthen me. Regardless of the uncomfortable places that I reside in during my process, I know that I am resting in your mighty hand. Thank you, Father.

In Jesus name I pray, Amen.

To my Beautiful Wife,

Congratulations on writing your first book. Your hard work and dedication to the process paid off.

I Love You
Husband-Alrick Williams

To Mom,

Great job on your first book mom.
I am very proud of you.
I hope your book touch lives
the way you touch mine.

I Love you
Son-Ajani Williams